Roots

Lynn Stone

Rourke
Publishing LLC
Vero Beach, Florida 32964

www.rourkepublishing.com

PHOTO CREDITS: All photos © Lynn Stone, except pg. 4 © alohaspirit; pg. 6 © Christine Balderas; pg. 7, 15 © Malcolm Romain; pg. 8 © Paul Roux; pg. 9 © Marje Cannon; pg. 12 © Jphn Sigler; pg 13 © Sgame; pg.16 © Donald Johansson; pg. 18 © Nico Smit; pg. 21 © Eric Foltz

Editor: Robert Stengard-Olliges

Cover design by: Nicola Stratford, bdpublishing.com

Library of Congress Cataloging-in-Publication Data

Stone, Lynn M.
  Roots / Lynn Stone.
     p. cm. -- (Plant parts)
  ISBN 978-1-60044-554-5 (Hardcover)
  ISBN 978-1-60044-694-8 (Softcover)
  1. Roots (Botany)--Juvenile literature. I. Title.
  QK644.S76 2008
  581.4'98--dc22
                           2007015157

Printed in the USA

CG/CG

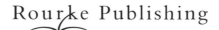

Rourke Publishing

www.rourkepublishing.com – rourke@rourkepublishing.com
Post Office Box 3328, Vero Beach, FL 32964

Table of Contents

Feet of Plants

Roots are the "feet" of plants. They reach down and keep plants firmly in place.

Roots usually grow from the lower part of a plant. Most roots grow in **soil**.

A root grows from one end
of a seed. A **stem** grows
from the other end.
    Stems typically grow
upward, toward the sun.
Leaves and flowers grow
from stems.

PARTS OF A PLANT

leaves

stem

seed

roots

7

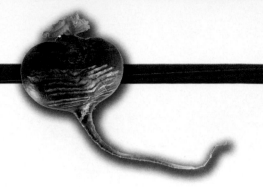

Roots generally grow downward. Some grow fairly deep into soil. Some grow shallow and spread out.

Absorbing Nutrients

Have you seen paper towels soak up water? This process is called **absorption**. Roots soak up **nutrients** from the soil and water. Nutrients are like vitamins for a plant.

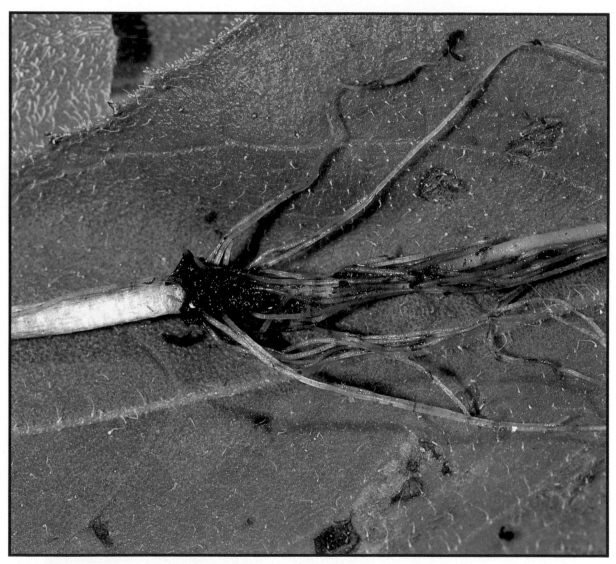

Root hairs do most of the absorption. Root hairs are not like animal hair. They have a different purpose. But they look like hair.

root hair

Some roots store food for plants. A carrot is the main root of a carrot plant. A carrot root is full of stored food. Turnips, beets, and sweet potatoes are roots, too.

15

Special Roots

Plants that live on trees have special roots. Their roots attach to tree **bark**. They absorb nutrients that reach the bark.

16

17

Mangroves have **prop roots** for extra support. Prop roots grow in soil and out of soil. They look like spider legs.

Mangroves need extra support to stand in the seashore mud.

19

Bald cypress tree roots grow "knees." These hard growths stick out above ground. The strange knees probably help support the tree in wet, swampy soil.

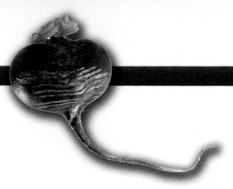

Glossary

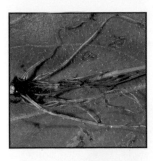

absorption (ab ZORP shuhn) — the process of soaking up

bark (BARK) — the hard covering on the outside of a tree

nutrients (NOO tree uhntz) — something that nourishes or makes healthy

prop roots (PROP RUTZ) — a
    support root growing partly
    above ground

stem (STEM) — the long, main part
    of a plant from which leaves and
    flowers grow

soil (SOYL) — dirt or earth in
    which plants grow

Index

Further Reading

Bodach, Vijaya. *Roots*. Pebble Plus, 2007.

Farndon, John. *Root*. Thomson Gale, 2006.

Mitchell, Melanie. *Roots*. First Avenue Editions, 2007.

Websites to Visit

www.kathimitchell.com/plants.html

www.urbanext.uiuc.edu/gpe/case1/c1facts2a.html

www.picadome.fcps.net/lab/currl/plants/default.htm

About the Author

Lynn M. Stone is the author of more than 400 children's books. He is a talented natural history photographer as well. Lynn, a former teacher, travels worldwide to photograph wildlife in its natural habitat.

MASKS

Lyndie Wright

Consultant: Henry Pluckrose

Photography: Chris Fairclough

FRANKLIN WATTS
London/New York/Sydney/Toronto

Copyright © 1990 Franklin Watts

Franklin Watts
387 Park Avenue South
New York
NY 10016

US ISBN: 0-531-14025-3

Design: K & Co
Editor: Jenny Wood

Printed in Belgium

Wright, Lyndie.
     Masks / Lyndie Wright.
          p.   cm. — (Fresh start)
     Summary: Provides step-by-step illustrated instructions for making
a variety of masks, including painted masks, balloon masks,
cardboard robot masks, and shadow masks.
     ISBN 0-531-10856-2
     1. Masks—Juvenile literature.   [1. Masks. 2. Handicraft.]
I. Title.   II. Series: Fresh start (London, England)
TT898.W75   1990
745.5—dc20   89-36533
                                                              CIP
                                                              AC

Contents

Equipment and materials

This book describes activities which use the following:

Adhesives (Elmer's glue for general use, a fabric glue such as "tacky" glue or "uniquestick" for cloth)

Balloons (round, and the size of your head when inflated)

Brushes (for glue and paints)

Calico (a type of cotton cloth)

Cane (pencil-thickness)

Cardboard

Cardboard boxes (you will need several of these)

Cloth (scraps)

Compasses (the mathematical drawing instrument type)

Dowel rods (or thin, flat sticks)

Elastic (hat elastic or thin, flat elastic)

Face paints or theatrical make-up

Feathers

Indian inks

Jam jars (old, for water)

Junk materials (e.g. cardboard tubes, toilet roll centers, egg boxes, yogurt cartons, bottle tops, cotton spools)

Kitchen knife (old, blunt)

Masking tape

Needle (large)

Net or muslin (scraps)

Newspaper

Paint (poster or tempera)

Paper (white, colored and crêpe)

Paper plates (large, white)

Pencils and/or pens

Plastic bucket or bowl (old)

Plastic food trays (old, for mixing paints)

Plastic fruit juice containers (large, empty)

Raffia

Reading lamp (with a 100-watt or 150-watt bulb)

Scissors

Shadow screen (an old, double bed sheet)

Silver paint (can be bought in liquid form)

String

Thread

Trimming knife

Water

Wool

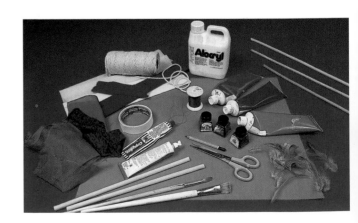

As well as being fun, making masks can be a simple and inexpensive task. The basic materials for the masks described in this book are cardboard boxes, balloons, newspaper and an old sheet. The decorations are made from throwaway household junk such as yogurt cartons, egg cartons and scraps of cloth and paper. The glues and paints are the only items you will need to buy, but you may even find that these are available at school or at home.

Keep a cardboard box at home and ask your family to put into it any clean plastic or cardboard containers they have finished with. You will find these very useful, and they may even give you good ideas for future masks.

Try making some of the masks in the earlier sections first, as you will find that the skills you learn there will help you as you go on to the more difficult masks further on in the book.

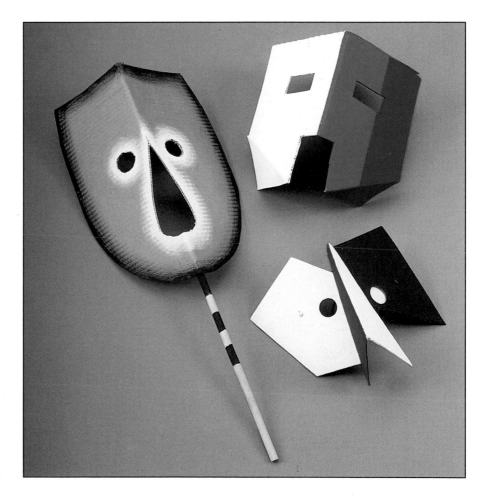

1 A selection of masks.

Proportions of the face

Before you start making masks, you should take some measurements to find out how your eyes, nose, mouth and ears lie in relation to each other and to the shape of your head.

If you measure an adult's head, you will find that the eyes are about halfway between the top of the head and the chin. If you measure a baby's head, you will notice that the eyes are somewhat lower down the head.

By the time people are nine or ten, their eyes are more or less midway.

Now measure the position of your nose. The end of the nose, you will notice, is about halfway between the eyes and the chin. The mouth is just above the halfway point between the end of the nose and the chin. The ears are usually situated between the level of the eyes and the bottom of the nose.

1 This is a rough but useful guide when drawing a head shape or making a mask.

Painted masks

You will need a large sheet of paper, a pencil or pen, poster or tempera paints, paintbrushes, water, plastic food trays for mixing the paint, and scissors.

Using the correct proportions for your own head, draw six mask heads on the sheet of paper. Color these, keeping the patterns and colors very simple. Poster or tempera paints will give you strong, clean colors.

1 Cut out the masks then cut out the eye holes. Hold the masks in front of your face one by one and look in a mirror to see the different effects each one gives.

Painted face with surround

You will need a large sheet of cardboard, a pencil or pen, scissors, a dowel rod or flat stick, glue, masking tape, poster or tempera paints, paintbrushes, water, plastic food trays for mixing the paint, crêpe or colored paper, and face paints or theatrical make-up.

1 Draw the outline of your face onto the center of the sheet of cardboard. Cut out the hole for your face. Decide on a shape for the face surround, draw it and then cut it out.

2 Fasten the dowel rod or flat stick onto the back of the surround with glue and masking tape.

3 Paint the surround and decorate it with crêpe or colored paper.

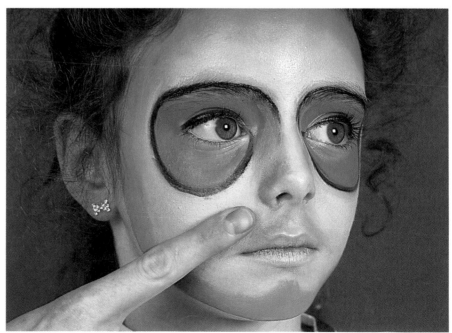

4 Paint your face with face paints to match the colors on the surround.

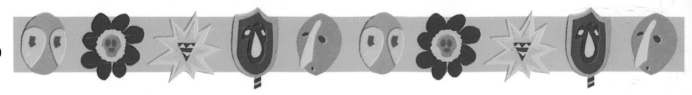

5 The colors and patterns of the face paints add to the effect of this sunburst surround.

6 This surround of orange petals and the matching face paints create a flower effect.

You will need three large white paper plates, a pencil or pen, scissors, scraps of cardboard, glue, poster or tempera paints, water, paintbrushes, and plastic food trays for mixing the paint.

1 On the first plate, draw and cut out the eyes, nose and mouth (or whichever features you wish to be cut away on your mask).

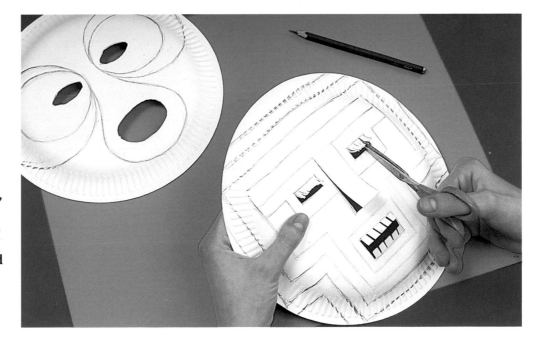

2 On the second plate, draw your chosen features. Cut the plate, but this time leave the cut cardboard attached so that it can be bent outwards to form eyelashes, nose and teeth.

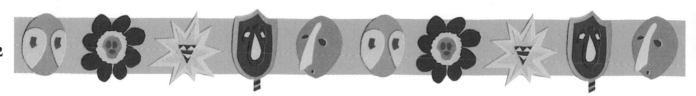

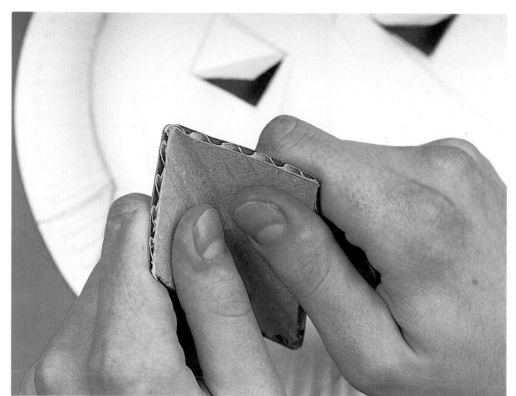

3 On the third plate, draw and cut out the eyes and mouth only (cut the shapes right out or leave the cardboard attached, as you prefer). To make a nose for this mask, fold a suitable piece of scrap cardboard in half and cut to shape.

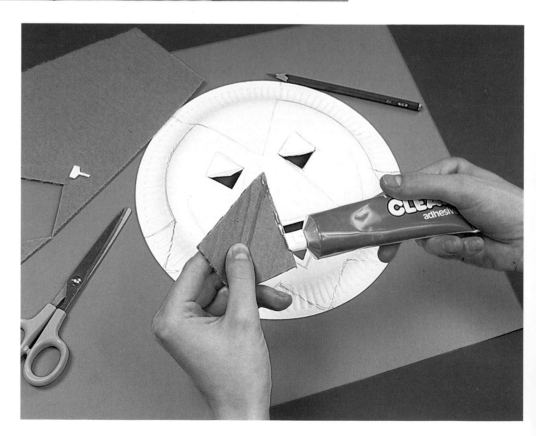

4 Squeeze a little glue on to the two sides of the cardboard nose which will touch the paper plate.

5 Press the nose firmly into position.

6 Paint your plate masks in such a way that the features stand out. If you want to wear the masks, attach some hat elastic to them (see page 44).

Flat cardboard masks

You will need a sheet of cardboard (or card from a cardboard box), a pencil or pen, scissors, glue, scraps of net or muslin, poster or tempera paints, paintbrushes, water, plastic food trays for mixing the paint, strips of colored paper, a blunt kitchen knife, a dowel rod or flat stick, and masking tape.

1 Cut out a piece of cardboard bigger than your face.

2 Draw and cut out large eye and mouth holes. Make a nose for the mask using a piece of scrap cardboard (see pages 12 and 13).

3 Cut pieces of net or muslin to fit over the eye and mouth holes, and glue these in position.

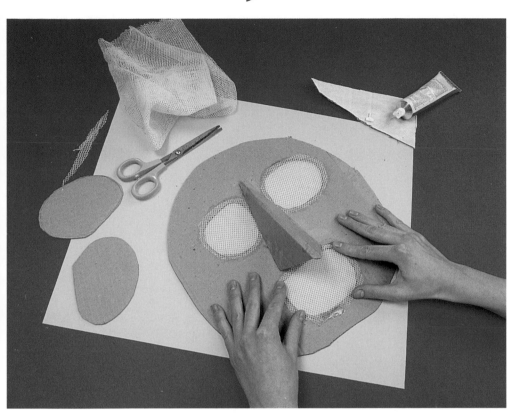

4 Paint your mask. Paint over the net as well as the cardboard with a dry brush so that you don't fill too many of the net holes with paint. When you hold the mask in front of your face, you will be able to see out but people will not be able to see you!

5 Make some hair for your mask from paper strips. You can make the strips curl by stretching them over the blade of a blunt knife. Pull and stretch in one movement. If they don't look curly enough, pull them over the knife a second time.

6 Glue the curled paper strips on to the back of the mask. Glue the dowel rod or stick to the back of the mask and secure with masking tape.

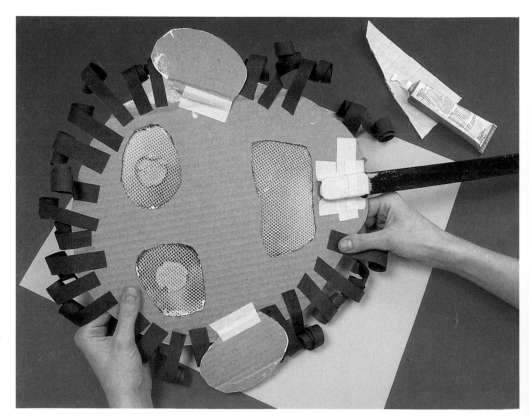

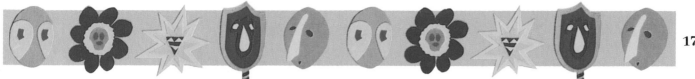

7 A completed mask in use. Always make sure your mask is facing the audience. If you hold it sideways it will seem to disappear.

Half-mask bird

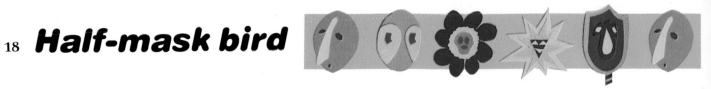

You will need two sheets of A3 paper, a pencil or pen, scissors, a cardboard box (one box will make two birds), glue, masking tape, poster or tempera paints, paintbrushes, water, plastic food trays for mixing the paint, elastic or string, and feathers or scraps of colored cloth or colored paper for plumage.

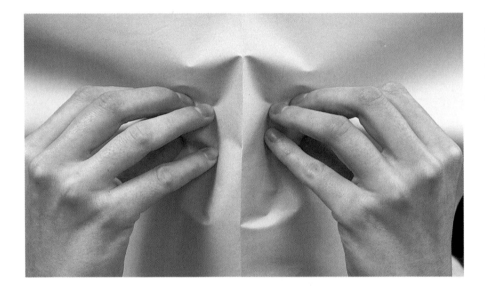

1 Fold one of the sheets of A3 paper in half and place it over your face. Feel where your eyes are and carefully mark their shape on the paper. Feel and mark a point halfway down your nose.

2 On the marked paper, draw a mask to cover the upper half of your face. Leave your mouth and chin exposed. Your mask should come down to the halfway point on your nose and should cover your cheek bones.

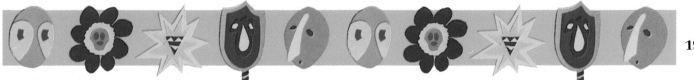

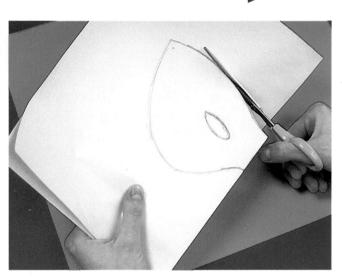

3 Cut out your paper pattern and fold it in half so that both sides are the same. Try it on and see if any alterations are necessary.

4 Place the paper pattern on a corner of the cardboard box and draw around it. Cut out the mask shape.

5 Fold the second piece of paper and cut out a beak. Try out one or two different beaks. Hold them against your mask to see which looks best. Trace your chosen beak onto another corner of the box and cut it out.

6 Glue the beak onto the mask and secure the join with masking tape.

7 Paint the beak and the eye surrounds. Fix on elastic or string ties (see page 44).

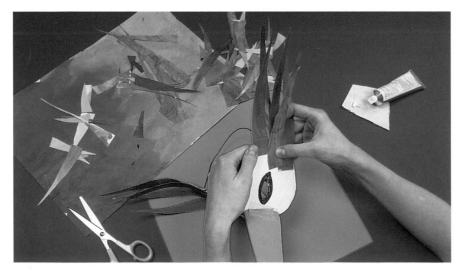

8 Cover the mask with real feathers or with feather-shaped pieces of cloth or painted paper. Start at the end furthest from the beak. Work towards the beak, making each new feather cover the base of the previous one.

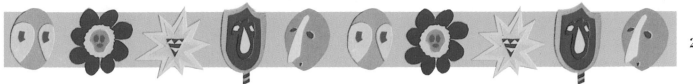

9 Three finished bird masks. The first has been covered with paper feathers, the second with real feathers and the third with cloth feathers.

Papier mâché masks

You will need old newspapers, an old plastic bucket or bowl, Elmer's glue, a cardboard box (one box will make four masks), a pencil or pen, scissors, elastic, poster or tempera paints, paintbrushes, water, plastic food trays for mixing the paint, string, wool or raffia for hair, and a trimming knife.

1 Tear up the old newspapers into small pieces about the size of postage stamps. Place these in the plastic bucket or bowl and soak them in water overnight.

2 Mash up the newspaper so that it looks like wet breadcrumbs. Now squeeze out as much water as you can and pour in some Elmer's glue. Work the glue into the newspaper, mashing with your fingertips. Keep the consistency fairly dry so that the paper mixture will hold a shape while being modeled.

3 Draw a full mask shape onto one corner of the cardboard box. The mask should be the length of your head and the width of your head from ear to ear. Cut out the mask shape.

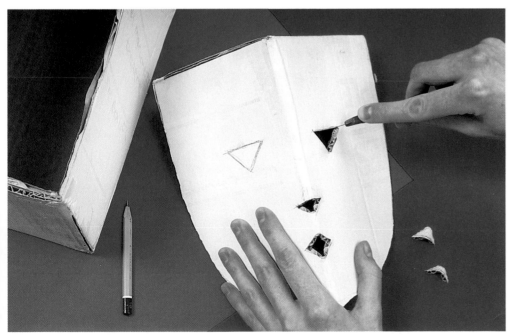

4 Measure the points where your eyes, nose and mouth are, and mark these on the mask. Cut out eye, nose and mouth holes. If you need to speak while wearing the mask, make sure that the mouth opening is large enough to let your voice out.

5 Build up the features on your mask with the papier mâché. When you have finished, leave the mask in a warm place to dry thoroughly.

6 When the mask is dry, make two holes at eye level and thread elastic through. Try your mask on and tie off the elastic when it feels comfortable. Now paint your mask. Add string, wool or raffia hair.

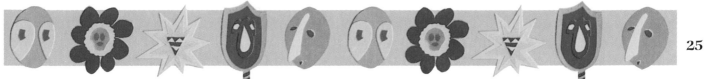

7 Two finished masks. One has hair made from painted string while the other has a wig and beard of raffia.

Balloon masks

You will need a round balloon (one balloon will make two masks), string, a cardboard tube, masking tape, Elmer's glue, an old jar for mixing the adhesive, water, a glue brush, newspaper (torn into small pieces), poster or tempera paints, paintbrushes, plastic food trays for mixing the paint, a pencil or pen, scissors, toilet roll centers, and hat elastic.

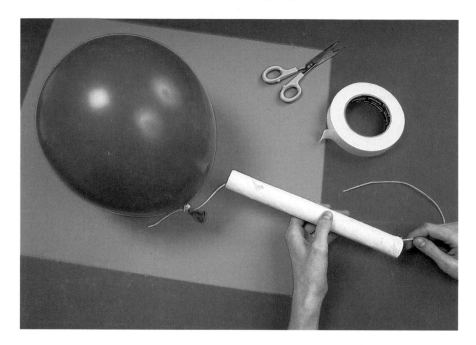

1 Blow up your balloon to headsize or a little bigger. Tie it tightly with a piece of string. Thread the string through the cardboard tube, pull it tight and secure the end with masking tape. This will make the balloon easier to hold during the next stage.

2 Pour some glue into the jar. Add an equal amount of water and mix thoroughly. Now cover the balloon with pieces of newspaper painted on both sides with the thinned adhesive. When you have completed one layer, mix a little paint in with some of the adhesive mix and do another layer. Alternate painted layers with clear layers three or four times. Be careful not to get the balloon too wet and soggy. When completed, leave to dry overnight.

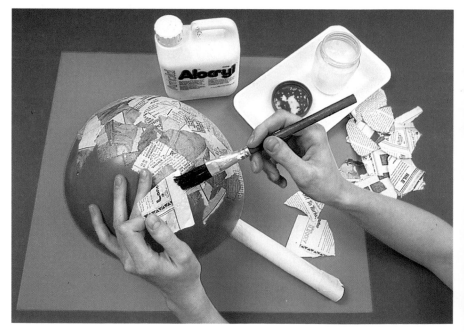

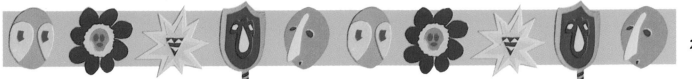

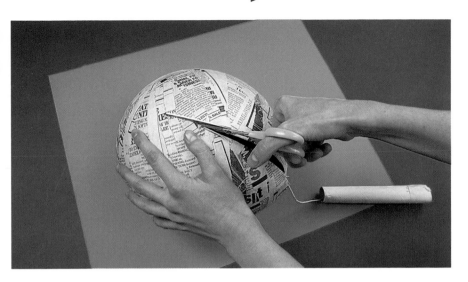

3 When the newspaper layers have dried, remove the cardboard tube and cut the covered balloon in half. You will now have two mask bases.

4 Mark the position of your eyes, and cut eye holes. Do the same for your nose and mouth if you need to.

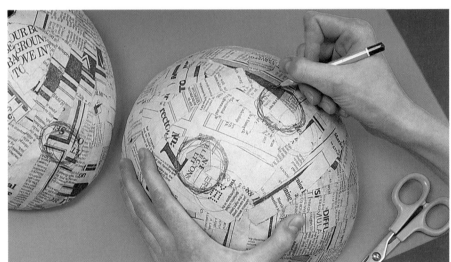

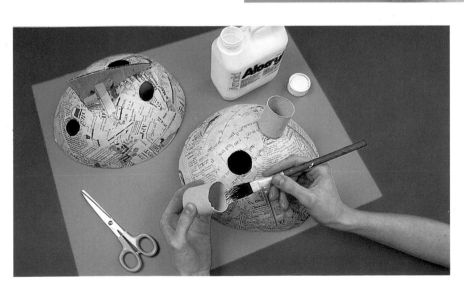

5 Make any additions you choose. Here, two toilet roll centers are being used for the eyes of the alien and a piece of cardboard for the nose of the other mask. Stick the features on with glue and cover the joins with glued newspaper pieces. Let dry for an hour.

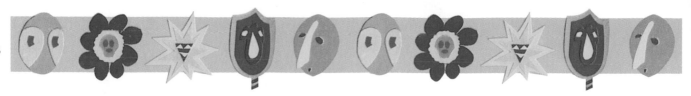

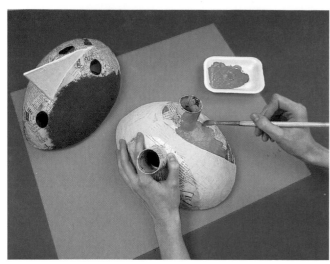

6 When the masks are dry, add elastic or string (see page 44) then paint them.

7 Two finished balloon masks.

Robot mask

This mask is made from throwaway household junk such as egg cartons, yogurt cartons, bottle tops, toilet roll centers and cotton reels.

You will also need a cardboard box (just big enough to fit over your head), a pencil or pen, scissors, poster or tempera paints, paintbrushes, water, plastic food trays for mixing the paint, silver paint, glue and masking tape.

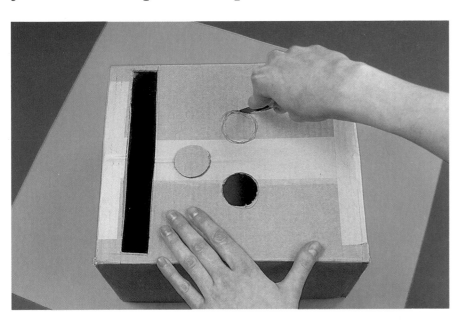

1 Put the cardboard box over your head and mark the positions of your eyes and mouth. Remove the box and cut eye and mouth holes. Cut a rounded hole at the bottom of the box for your neck.

2 Gather together a collection of junk materials to decorate your robot mask.

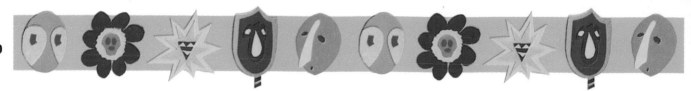

3 Using these junk materials, add features to your mask. Here, a large egg carton has been used for the mouth and an egg carton top with two yogurt cartons sitting on it for the eyes. The centers of the yogurt cartons and the egg carton top have been cut away for looking through. Sections of egg cartons have been used to represent large bolts, and toilet roll centers have been stuck on for ears and hair.

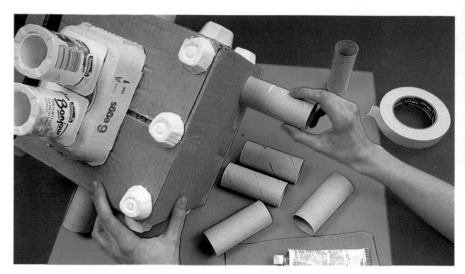

4 Finally, the entire mask has been painted with dark gray paint. A "metallic" look has been created by adding highlights of silver paint.

You could add all sorts of features to your robot mask. You could even try making a cardboard-box body for your robot.

You will need a large cardboard box, a pencil or pen, scissors or a trimming knife, a pair of compasses, masking tape, a thin-handled paintbrush, scraps of cotton cloth, elastic, a cardboard egg carton, glue, poster or tempera paints, paintbrushes, water, plastic food trays for mixing the paint, a dowel rod or flat stick, and colored paper.

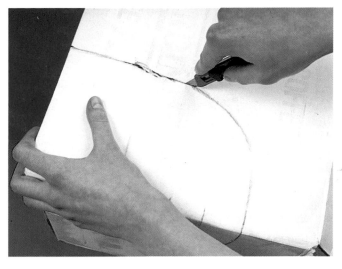

1 Draw the mask head on to a corner of the cardboard box. The mask should be the length of your head and the width of your head from ear to ear. Cut out the mask shape.

2 Cut away the nose and mouth area completely, leaving the cheek pieces. These will hold the lower beak. Cut out eye holes.

3 On a second corner of the box, draw the upper beak. The total width of this feature needs to be about 11in (5½in on each side of the box corner). Cut out the beak then cut away a section at the top (about 2in down the fold) so that the beak sits comfortably on the mask. (NB In the drawing, the cutting lines are shown as dotted lines.) The beak can be as long as you like. The one in these pictures is 13in long.

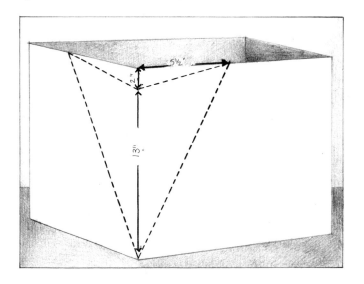

4 Draw and cut out the lower beak in the same way. This time draw a circle with a radius of 1in on each of the ends which will fix on to the mask. These will be attached with a moving joint, at a later stage.

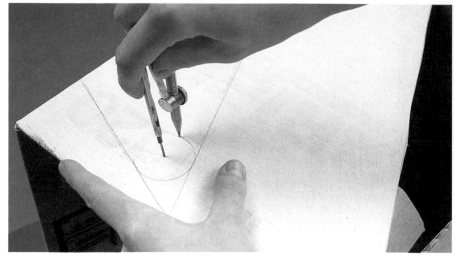

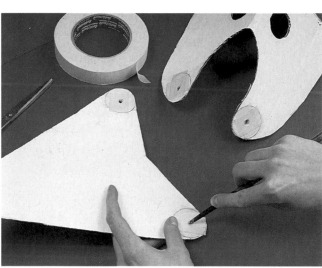

5 Reinforce these circle areas with two or three pieces of masking tape and pierce a hole through the center of each with the handle of the thin-handled paintbrush. Make two circles of the same size on the jaw ends of the mask. Reinforce these with masking tape and pierce a hole through each, exactly as for the lower beak. Gently bend these circles in towards the face and bend the lower beak circles outwards.

6 Cut two strips of cotton cloth, each 1.5in wide, to use as joints. Thread each strip through one of the lower beak holes and its matching mask hole. Tie a knot at each end of each strip.

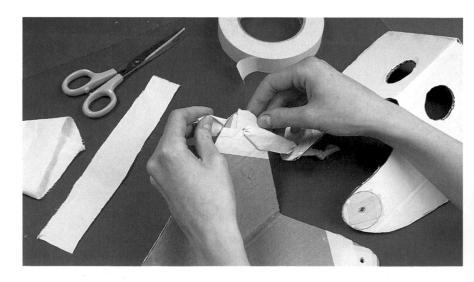

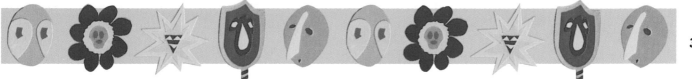

7 Stick these knots down with masking tape to stop them pulling through.

8 Attach the upper beak to the mask with masking tape. To attach the mask to your head, fix on elastic as shown on page 44.

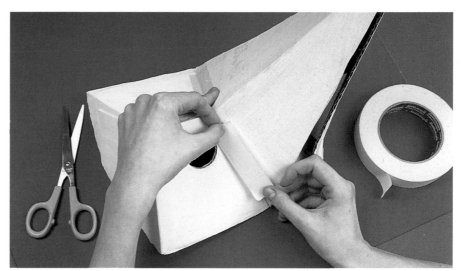

9 Eyelids can be made from the "cups" of an egg carton. Glue these in position. Now paint your mask and decorate it with feathers cut from painted or colored paper.

10 If you would like to be able to control the mouth movement, attach the dowel rod or flat stick to the lower beak with masking tape and work it with one of your hands in time to your speech.

Plastic masks

You will need various large plastic containers of the kind used for holding fruit juice or other liquids. Ask your school cafeteria or local restaurant for empty ones. Don't use any container you are unsure of as it may have held liquids which are poisonous or dangerous to the skin. Wash the container thoroughly before you start, otherwise you may find yourself covered with sticky juice. You will also need scissors.

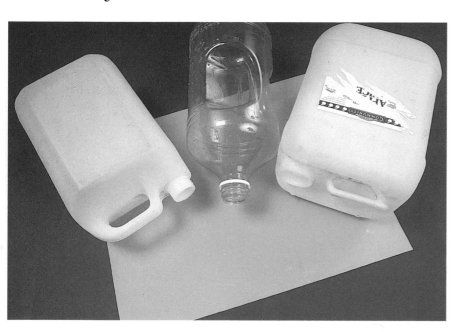

1 These containers will make excellent masks. Turn them around to see what shapes and characters they suggest to you.

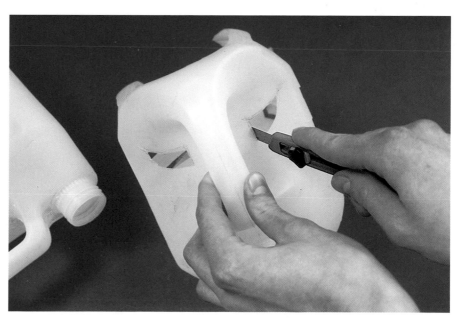

2 Most plastic containers are very easy to cut with scissors. If you find a tough one, ask an adult to help you by cutting it with a trimming knife.

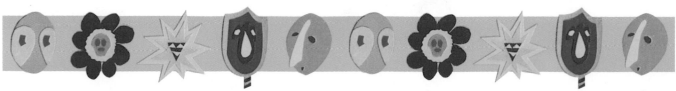

3 A selection of finished plastic masks. One has curls which have been rolled around a stick and then left to uncurl. There is no need to paint plastic masks, as they catch the light well just as they are.

Cane and calico body mask

You will need 3-4 yards of cane (pencil-thickness), masking tape, cardboard, scissors, elastic, glue, 1.5 yards of 36in-wide calico (or an old sheet), a large needle and thread, scraps of net, scraps of colored material for hair, poster paints or Indian inks, paintbrushes, water, and plastic food trays for mixing the paint or inks.

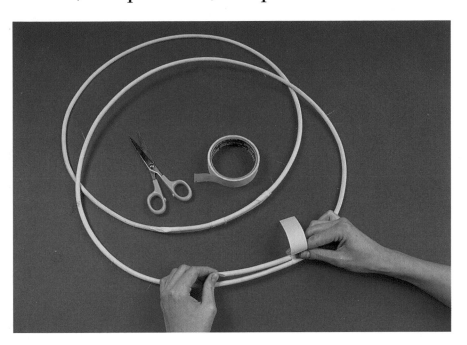

1 Gently bend some of the cane to make two circles big enough to pass comfortably over your shoulders (you will need about 62in of cane for each circle). Join the ends of the cane together with masking tape.

2 Next, you need to make an attachment to fit onto your head. On one of the circles make a cross of cane and fasten it with masking tape. Cut a strip of cardboard 3in wide and long enough to make a circle which will sit comfortably on top of your head. Join the cardboard circle to the cane cross with masking tape. Try it on. If it feels wobbly, tie some elastic onto the cross to fit under your chin (just as you might do with a hat).

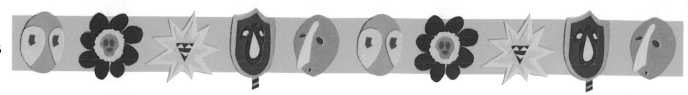

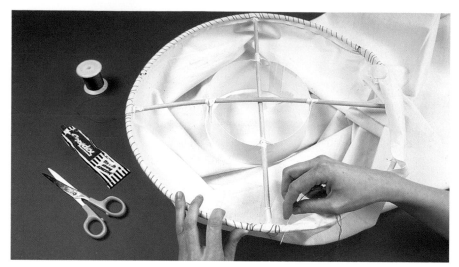

3 Glue one of the long sides of the piece of calico round the cane circle which has the head attachment. For extra strength, sew the calico and the cane together with big stitches. These stitches will be covered up later, so they don't have to be very neat.

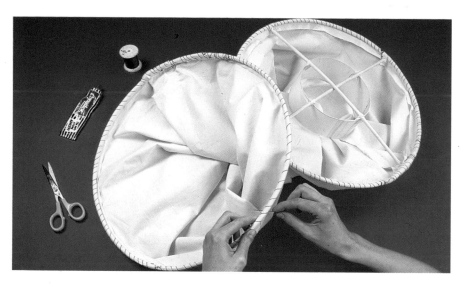

4 Glue and/or sew the second cane circle to the other long end of calico, making the whole thing into a cylinder shape. Sew together the two sides of the calico that run down the length of the cylinder. This join will be at the back of the body mask.

5 Put the calico cylinder over your head and get your teacher or another adult to cut two slits for your arm holes. Each of these slits should be about 12in long and should run straight down the sides of the cylinder. If you are going to use your body mask a lot, oversew these slits to stop them tearing further.

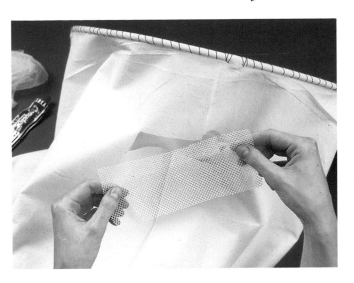

6 Mark the position of your eyes on the calico cylinder. Take off the cylinder and cut an eye slot about 6in wide and 2in deep. Cut a piece of net to fit over the hole and glue it in position. You will now be able to see out, but other people won't be able to see in!

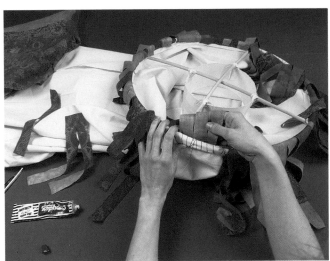

7 Cut strips of colored material for hair and stick these on to the top of the cylinder.

8 Hang your body mask from a doorway or get someone to wear it while you decorate the face with colored inks or paint.

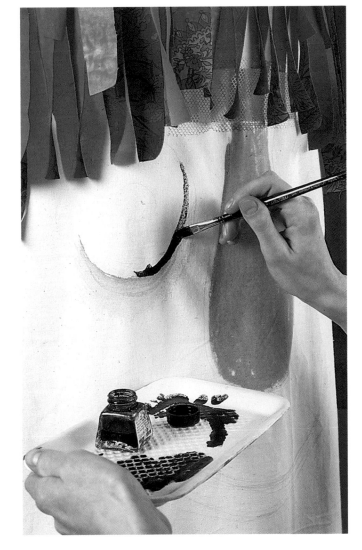

9 A completed cane and calico body mask.

You could use your body mask in a carnival parade, but be sure that you have someone beside you to guide you safely. *This is particularly important if you are walking along roads where there is traffic.*

Shadow masks

Have you ever held a shadow show, with your hands making rabbits and other shapes on a wall? Now you can try a whole body shadow show, with your head disguised by a shadow mask!

Hang a large sheet (a double bed sheet would be ideal) across a double doorway, or suspend it from the ceiling on a pole. Get a teacher or another adult to help you hang it. Remember: the audience must be on the unlit side of the sheet and you, the shadow, must be on the lit side.

Point a reading lamp with a 100-watt or 150-watt bulb at your side of the screen and work between it and the screen. The effects can be magical.

You will need large sheets of cardboard (as thick as possible, but make sure you can cut the cardboard with scissors), scissors, masking tape, glue, and dowel rods or flat sticks for reinforcing bending cardboard.

1 Measure the length and the width of your head. Now draw a head shape, larger than your own, onto a piece of cardboard. If it is large enough, you could even cut out an eye.

2 Cut out the head and eye that you have drawn.

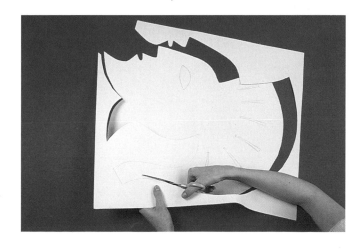

3 Add a loop of cardboard to fit around your head. Glue this loop in position and secure with masking tape.

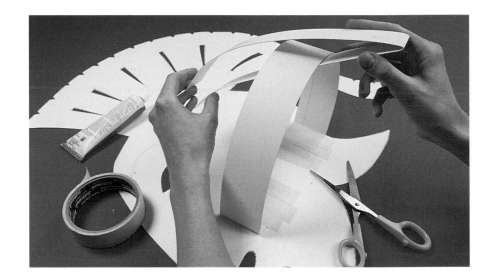

4 Now fold a second strip of cardboard in half and thread it through the first loop.

5 Glue this strip of cardboard in position and secure with masking tape. Your mask should now fit quite securely onto your head. If the cardboard seems inclined to bend, reinforce it with a dowel rod or stick or even a scrap of cardboard.

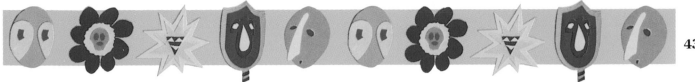

Now work out the action of the show, remembering to keep your mask facing the audience. Keep your actions slow and clear. You will find the results very exciting.

6 Cut out props to help you with your action or story. The Grecian soldiers here have been given swords and shields.

How to fasten your masks

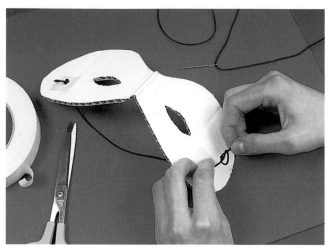

1 *Elastic*
Elastic is the most convenient way of attaching a mask. The elastic will go around the back of your head and be fixed to the mask at eye level. Reinforce with masking tape the area of cardboard where the elastic joins. Thread the elastic through the mask, tie a double knot and stick the knot down with another piece of tape. Hat elastic or thin, flat elastic are best.

2 *String*
Fix two pieces of string to your mask in the same way as you would fix elastic. The mask can now be tied on behind your head.

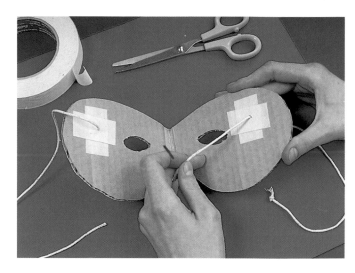

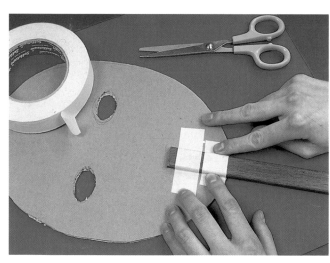

3 *Held stick*
This allows you to change from face to mask or from mask to mask quickly. Glue a dowel rod or flat stick to your mask and reinforce the join with masking tape.

4 *Cardboard loops*
Take care when putting on and taking off the mask, or you may pull off the loops. Measure the card strips carefully. Glue in position and secure with masking tape.

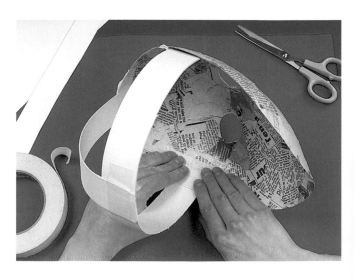

Museums

The museums listed display a variety of masks: if you have a particular interest or are looking for something special, you might want to call a museum before going there to be sure their collection has what you want. Another good idea is to call the museums in your area – if they do not have masks or the type of mask you're looking for, they may be able to direct you to a collection that does. Also, if there is a local children's museum you can call them and ask if they offer workshops or any other activities on mask making.

American Museum of National History
79 Central Park West
New York, New York
(212) 769-5100
        769-5000

Brooklyn Children's Museum
145 Brooklyn Avenue
Brooklyn, New York
(718) 735-4400

Herrd Museum
22 E. Monta Vista Road
Phoenix, Arizona
(602) 252-8440

Institute of the Arts
5200 Woodward Avenue
Detroit, Michigan
(313) 833-7900

Smithsonian Institution
African Art Museum
1050 Independence Avenue, S.W.
Washington, D.C.
(202) 357-1300

Smithsonian Institution
Museum of Natural History
10th Street and Constitution Avenue, N.W.
Washington, D.C.
(202) 357-1300

Books to read

HALLOWEEN MASKS by Anthony Rao, 1984: Random House

MASKS AND MASK MAKERS by Karl Hunt and Bernice W. Carlson. 1960: Abingdon.

MASKS AND PUPPETS by Louise Nevette. 1984: Franklin Watts.

Material suppliers

Stationers and/or arts and crafts stores will stock the majority of the adhesives and paints listed in this book, as well as specialized materials. Materials in large quantities can often be purchased or ordered through these same stores or school suppliers – you can ask if there are any catalogs available.

Theatrical makeup and face paints are available at some arts and crafts stores and costume shops

A brief history of masks

Masks of worship

Many thousands of years ago, our ancestors were already aware of the power of the mask. In the south of France, in caves used for religious ceremonies, they made paintings of the animals they hunted, among which are the first tentative drawings of people. In these drawings the figures are shown wearing animal masks. A hunter, to give himself courage and to get into the spirit of the animal he wished to hunt, would wear the mask of that animal and would enact the scene of the kill he hoped to bring about. This is still done today among some hunting tribes of the world as far apart as Africa and Alaska.

In ancient Egypt, animal masks were used to represent the spirits of the dead. In Africa and in the South Pacific islands, masks are still used for this purpose. The people there believe that the spirits of their dead are very important and, through the power of the mask, can be called upon to help in the growing of crops, in the calling up of rain and in protection from enemies and illness.

The ancient Egyptians also made human masks. These were used in tombs to protect the dead from demons in their after-life. Death masks were used too in the ancient civilisations of China, Mexico and Peru.

In Sri Lanka, masks represent the spirits of sickness. Ritual mask dancing drives out these spirits, so the illness may be cured.

Masks were important in the fertility rites of ancient Europe. These rites were abolished with the coming of Christianity, but fertility masks are still used in inaccessible areas of Europe such as the mountain villages of Switzerland and Austria.

All over the world, in different cultures and at different times, the mask has given people the courage to face the known as well as the unknown forces in their lives.

Performance masks

The earliest theater as we know it began in Greece in the 5th century B.C. Before this, ritual dramas were sung and danced by a chorus, with a narrator telling a story based on the legends of the gods.

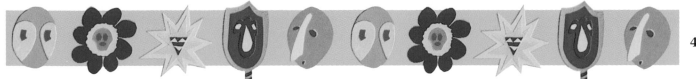

Eventually a poet by the name of Thespis of Athens wrote a play, giving the storyteller the task of speaking in dialogue. To make it easier for the audience to tell which character was speaking at a particular time, the narrator used different masks to represent the various characters. These plays were performed in natural amphitheaters on the hillsides and, to make the narrator's voice travel over the whole area, the masks were given large funnel-shaped mouths like megaphones. (The Greek word for an actor is "hypocrites". So our word, hypocrite, is derived from the fact that an actor wore a mask and was "two-faced".)

The Romans borrowed the Greeks' ideas of theater, including their use of masks. But, as often happens with borrowed things, they lost their vigor. So the Romans added sensational effects such as wild animals fighting to the death. They even filled the Colosseum, their great amphitheater in Rome, with water and performed great sea battles there. All this was eventually abandoned with the fall of the Roman Empire.

In Italy, in the 16th century, a new, exciting style of theater called the Commedia dell'Arte began. The actors were masked, but with half masks so that the audience could see changes in the actors' expressions. A Commedia dell'Arte play had no written script, only a rough plot. The actors each played a set character whom they studied and believed in so strongly that, when any situation arose, they knew exactly how that character would react.

These characters, known as "zanni", were favorites in Europe for over 200 years and have never really been forgotten: Punch, Harlequin and Pierrot are their direct descendants.

In the East, masks have always had a place of great importance in the theater while in many western parts of the world masks have simply become a form of disguise – something with which to hide faces and give a touch of excitement to carnivals, masked balls and Halloween. But don't treat your mask too lightly, for it has had a very powerful past! And who knows where it may take you now?

PRINTED IN BELGIUM BY
proost
INTERNATIONAL BOOK PRODUCTION